CURFEW OVER THE MOSS

TALES OF HALSALL CHURCH FROM MEDIEVAL TIMES TO THE PRESENT

Stephen Henders

Countyvise Ltd

First Published 2014 by Countyvise Ltd
14 Appin Road, Birkenhead, CH41 9HH

British Library Cataloguing in Publication Data.
A catalogue record for this book is available from the British Library.

ISBN 978 1 906823 99 3

To my Angels
who, at the moment of my despair,
came in legion.

The Curfew bell was rung about eight o'clock in the evening, in medieval times and like the Angelus bell it marked the hours for the villagers. Derived from the French 'couvre feu' it signalled the need to dampen down the fire before they went to sleep. The Curfew bell was also rung during fogs and mists to guide travellers on the moss and marsh land around Halsall guiding them to a safe haven.

Preface

A building built for devotion may often inspire devotion in different ways. A church inspires devotion to God, in whose name the church was constructed with love, care and copious hard work. There is also the devotion and care given by ordinary people over centuries to care for preserve and ornate the church. It is all of these qualities which compelled me to write a series of articles about this magnificent medieval structure and the parish in which it is positioned.

Inside and outside of these esteemed walls, the old stones have overseen and eavesdropped on great events over 700 years. These events range from the tragedy of the Black Death to the glory of Agincourt, through the Reformation, the Armada and the Restoration; right up to the two great conflicts of the 20th century. Without and within the walls dead from several wars have been buried and commemorated. The stones have reflected the fires and bombs of the blitz of the Second World War as villagers feared for the future like so often and so many before them. I have tried where possible to give a grass roots viewpoint, that is, the perspective of the common people at the time. I have included in this the importance of the parish church throughout the ages for the villager, not just as a place of worship but as the centre of village life.

There is also a chronological order leading up to contemporary time. Most of the articles are factual, but there is some fictional licence mingled with historical fact. I have done this to better illustrate a situation. The articles have been written over a period of fifteen years and collected here; I hope they will serve as a historical reference for generations to come.

Stephen Henders

Acknowledgements

I wish to thank Paul the Rector for his interest and for permission to publish the articles in the local magazine Halsall News. Thanks also to the churchwardens David Sephton and Brian Heaton for allowing me to wander all over the church and into nooks and crannies undisturbed since medieval times. A grateful thanks to the many Halsall folk who gave me stories and anecdotes. John Phillips, friend and published author, kindly proof read the work and gave much valuable advice. Finally to my devoted and much loved wife Ann for her encouragement and help in every way.

Stephen Henders

*All profits from the sale of this book will go
towards the repair of the church spire.*

Contents

Foreword

St Cuthbert's Church is a fine, ancient church in the Lancashire Village of Halsall. The church attracts interest from people far and wide as it is now on a fairly busy road taking people to Southport to the north and Liverpool to the south. St Cuthbert's is an amazing building with lots of 'nooks and crannies' to explore, and of course a great deal of history is attached to the building, and as I'm sure you can imagine many stories and myths are told about this ancient church and its environs.

Stephen Henders who knows the church and churchyard well has put together in one volume many of the articles he has previously printed in the 'Halsall News Letter'. I have found the book a very enjoyable, and historically valuable, read and am delighted that he has put it together. As you read it, I am sure that, like me, you will be transported back to another time, when this ancient church was at the centre of a 'little village'. You will also enjoy the many 'tales and curiosities' that are connected and attributed to this special building that still today is held in great esteem by so many, many people.

I am happy to commend this book to you and thank Stephen for all his hard work in putting it together.

Enjoy it for yourself.

The Revd Paul Robinson
Rector

SECTION I

700 YEARS OF HISTORY

Halsall Church washed by evening rain

Halsall a Medieval History

When Henry VIII broke with Rome and declared himself head of the church in England in 1535, it was a major event in the history of our country. It also had a profound effect on the local area and the parish church which is one of only a handful of churches, in the south west Lancashire region, which predate the Reformation of the 16th century. We know that Lancashire and particularly the seaboard side of Lancashire clung on stubbornly and devoutly to the Old Faith of Catholicism. The Reformation here was a slow and reluctant process, not least because Tudor Lancashire was in many parts poor and totally reliant on farming. It was also just far enough away from London and York to be a quite isolated part of the realm lying within the diocese of Lichfield which was 100 miles away. We have very little firsthand evidence of what life was like for the people of Halsall and surrounding villages but we do know that given the fervent faith in religion, the edifice of St Cuthbert's was central to the lives of this agricultural community. In the next few pages we are going to examine the fabric of the building, the traditions, customs, faith and belief up to and beyond the Reformation and look at the profound change in the way of life this had for local people.

The building of a parish church, in dressed stone, with a tower was a singular work of devotion to God but was also a statement of the wealth and status of the locals who embellished it. The Norman foundations suggest a church had been built on this site before the present structure, but it may well have been wooden. The construction of the present building began in 1320 but the Black Death in 1349 resulted in construction of the church being halted in the 14th century. In the 150 years before the Reformation two thirds of churches in England saw substantial reconstruction on a lavish scale. Halsall was included in this and the work on the new chancel was to make it one of the most beautiful in England. Halsall served a large agricultural area mainly based on crop rotation and some herding, with a nearby ready market in Ormskirk. It was like all 14th century churches, under the jurisdiction of the Pope.

Let us try and picture the typical parish scene in pre Reformation Halsall. Here was a farming and manorial community in which many features of the old feudal system persisted and the great families held sway over the local people. Attending the parish church was an essential part of belonging to the community. In pre-reformation Halsall you were compelled by God and social custom to attend Mass on Sunday and on the holy days. The community adhered to the calendar for the Liturgical year, which was dictated by the seasons and which determined the times of fast and feast. The Angelus bells and Curfew bells were rung from the church at the appointed hours and signalled to the workers in the fields the times to rest, the times to eat and the times to pray; essentially ringing out the hours like a clock.

The year's work was punctuated by holy days according to the Sarum calendar days of veneration to God and His saints. Plough ceremonies most probably started the farming year in February. On Rogation day 25th April it was the custom to go in procession through the parish with bells and litanies sung to the saints marking out the parish boundaries in prayer and ceremony. The most elaborate ceremonies took place at Eastertide, Christmas and Candlemas. The richness of the carol tradition we enjoy today has come down to us from the medieval period. Easter began on Palm Sunday with elaborate and devout ceremonies. It continued with Tenebrae in Holy Week, an intense period of prayer and denial lasting until Good Friday a day of mourning and fasting. Rituals such as creeping to the cross on knees or bare feet were usual practices. Then a watch would be kept all weekend at the Easter sepulchre where the consecrated Host was put on display early on Easter Sunday morning. At Halsall Church the watch window built into the stairwell is located in the chancel. However the year was not confined only to the feasts which occur in winter and spring. There was a plethora of saint's days and holy days punctuating the whole year providing opportunity for devotion, feast, fast and holiday. Each church gave devotion to its own particular saints. It is likely that the popular saints in Halsall were St Cuthbert, St Oswald, St Nicholas, St Katherine, St Michael, St Helen and St Winifred. St Katharine and St Michael were popular saints in the 15th century. There still exists two medieval buildings contemporary at that time; the private chapel at Lydiate and the church at Aughton were dedicated to St Katharine and St Michael respectively. Sefton church and the well close by, visited by local pilgrims, were dedicated to St Helen. Similarly, the well in Holywell dedicated to St Winifride was more easily accessible than Canterbury and was being visited as a Catholic shrine by Nicholas Blundell 200 years later when the penal laws against Catholics were at their harshest. St Apollonia would have often been the target of intercession as the saint for toothache and there was much devotion to the Blessed Virgin. We know that two chantry chapels at St Cuthbert's were dedicated to St Nicholas patron of the sea and The Blessed Virgin. St Nicholas even had a statue in a niche at the point of the church furthest west and closest to the sea.

The St Nicholas Niche

The altar and Chancel were separated from the nave by a great intricately carved wooden screen. This was the rood screen and had a platform on top on which a figure of Christ on the cross attended by his mother and St John was in place. On the rood loft, plays and other displays of devotion were performed especially at Easter and on the feast of Corpus Christi. These were illuminated by the clerestory window and rood lights, which were candles, permanently lit on the structure. Plays were a fundamental means of transmitting religious instruction and stirring devotion but were suppressed from 1560 onwards by the reforms. Mass was often performed on the rood loft and an altar slab was found in the turret access during renovations in 1876. The access to the rood platform is still there in Halsall to this day aa well as the markings on the chancel arch where the great screen would have been held by heavy iron fasteners. It is likely that the church walls would have been brightly painted with scenes from Christ's life and possibly the Old Testament. Along with the stained glass windows, the carvings and statues, the illiterate agricultural villagers could interpret bible stories and be educated. The seven deadly sins were often carved on the exterior stonework of churches in form of gargoyles and Halsall church displays these torments to remind people what awaited them in Hell.

Printing had begun a hundred years before the Reformation and prayer books called primers as well as books of hours were available for the wealthy, with prayers in English for those who could read. Music also was composed by some of England's greatest composers Thomas Tallis and William Byrd wrote pieces for use in mass for four or five voice choirs. It is conjecture, however, to wonder if polyphony of this splendour was used at Halsall but plainchant would have undoubtedly been normal accompaniment before the Reformation.

In the medieval pre reformation era belief in God was unquestioned and people were at least outwardly pious. The great cycle of festival and devotion which took place in Halsall and other parishes of England were the key to the meaning of the parishioners' lives.

Elaborate religious ceremonies took place throughout Europe and if we consider the Semana Santa (holy week) processions which take place in many Spanish cities to this very day, where canopies are carried by villagers slowly through the streets, adorned with candles and flowers, we have an insight, though on a smaller scale, of the celebrations that took place in many English villages in medieval England. Halsall's Easter Sepulchre is testimony to this time of devotion and display. Situated on the north side of the chancel, the consecrated host was taken from the main altar and displayed there surrounded with flowers and candlelight. Statues and images topped the plinths and paintings richly adorned the sepulchre wall. The consecrated host would be on display on Easter Sunday following an elaborate ceremony shortly after midnight on Saturday. Here too it is likely that the host and images were carried in procession with decorated canopies on the village roads perhaps as far as some of the many medieval crosses which punctuated the wayside 'en route' for the Church.

The extent to which local parishioners contributed in time and effort to enhancing their church cannot be understated. The rich and poor saw it as their bounden duty to provide for the church as a measure of their devotion. Great satisfaction would have been afforded the parishioner with their offering and it gave them esteem and value within the community. As well as lavishly decorating the church, the community contributed by providing much of the furniture, vestments and ornaments involved with the services and clergy. A poor parishioner may not have been able to provide a jewelled chalice but could provide an altar cloth or simply candles to be lit before images as their pious contribution to the church.

When, because of the reforms, lights before images were banned along with the ringing of the Angelus and recitation of the Rosary, these changes struck at the very heart of the routine and harmony of the ordinary people. When holydays were abrogated by the Act in 1536 it was a curb on freedom of leisure and personal devotion to local saints. It was the cults of the saints, relics and the great emphasis on annual celebrations of feast days with the flowers, the music, the candles and bells which gave colour and vigour to people's life and worship. It gave purpose to community to work, to rest, to pray and to play.

However, these changes may not have been immediate in Halsall. By 1541 a new diocese had been formed with Chester as the Cathedral Church which incorporated Halsall. John Bird was the first bishop. He complained how backward his region was, "Popish idolatry is longer to continue in diver's colleges and places, idols are taken down but kept to worship" William Downham, his successor, was weak in enforcing religious penal laws, which were designed to compel Catholics to attend the Church of England services and fined them if they didn't comply. By 1547 Edward VI had ordered the dissolution of the chantries (small chapels). Halsall had two chantries, one dedicated to the Blessed Virgin on the north side and another to St Nicholas on the south. Well to do families would have these chantries dedicated to a deceased loved one and often paid a chantry priest to say mass and prayers for their soul for years and sometimes decades to come. In 1590 the situation of reform had in many ways remained static. The 'de profundis' bell was still rung for the dead, Rogantide rituals were also untouched 'though the Protestants ridiculed this as charming the fields'. Protestantism was a long time in making headway in South West Lancashire and where it did it was tempered and transformed.

When the desecration of relics, images and decoration was in full sway, at the height of the Reformation, there was no violent smashing of artefacts at Halsall. At some point however the Rood screen was dismantled and colourful paintings were whitewashed away. St Nicholas would have been taken down from his niche in the south west wall and perhaps smashed or more likely taken back into the home of a villager, who wished to remain faithful to the old ways. Images were removed, the chantry chapels were closed, the bells stopped. The physical evidence shows no great Protestant fervour to rid the church of images and artifacts. The hand raised in Benediction above the altar at the east end of the chancel is precisely the target for reformist zealots yet this is intact.

There was a reluctant and slow moving conformity. How late after the Reformation's first moves to proselytise the church did it take? We might consider the lack of conformity in Lancashire as a whole and given the agricultural nature of the parishioners and the wide spread of the parish, it may have been as late as the middle or end of Elizabeth's reign.

The Reformation and subsequent puritan philosophies brought a drabness and austerity which lingers to this day. The Church of England has, since the Restoration in 1660 of Charles II, reinstated in its own way many of the pre reformation traditions. The services perpetuated today in the church, Matins and Evensong were originally Catholic services. The bells, the candles the rituals have all been reinstated. Ironically the music of great Catholic composers of the 16th century is more often heard in Anglican Cathedrals than Roman Catholic ones. These masterpieces were written for 'a capella' performance in medieval buildings. All the medieval places of worship were sequestrated by the Church of England. Catholic Cathedrals in this country are always quite contemporary constructions. Somehow, the music of England's most glorious musical heritage can seem sometimes out of place in concrete chambers yet finds wonderful expression in the great stone medieval cathedrals.

The Easter Sepulchre

The Malevolent Curate

Gargoyle arms raised

The County History compiled in the Victorian era and available in Ormskirk library contains a lively account of an episode in our church's history concerning an errant curate. This episode occurred at a crucial time for the church of St Cuthbert because it was the start of the reforms set in motion by Henry VIII. Richard Halsall had been rector since 1513 and his brother Thomas Halsall was lord of the manor. Richard was an Oxford man and an academic whose desire to further his theological studies led him away from Halsall in 1530. We can speculate that he saw an opportunity to debate the new reforms. It was during his time at University that the conduct of his curate Thomas Kirkby became the subject of an appeal to the Chancellor of the Duchy by Thomas Halsall, lord of the manor, on behalf of himself and the inhabitants of Halsall

With the Rector gone, Thomas Kirkby began to exploit his position as the leading churchman in the parish. A curate's income was not lavish and in performing many of the rector's duties, Kirkby thought himself entitled to tithes and income from cattle which belonged to the Rector. It was also probable that the extent of the reforms affected the normal income for curates such as 'mortuaries'. This was a payment for saying the funeral masses and reciting prayers afterwards for the soul. The curate could expect a contribution from the mourners to continue these prayers for a set time. The reformers frowned upon these practices and legislated against them. The consequence was that Kirkby went to great lengths in the pulpit to describe how the recently deceased were languishing in Purgatory and Hell and suffering terrible fires, much to the upset of the recently bereaved villagers. Such insensitivity led to verbal clashes within the village, where Kirkby was involved in shouting matches and arguments calling people knaves and other ungodly names before taking himself into the church to perform mass. He embroiled himself in all church affairs and went around the village visiting the sick and persuading them to make their will and telling them they were bound to leave him something. He used his office to secure pecuniary advantage at every opportunity. He also used the time that the Rector was away to exact petty revenges against the villagers. Indeed it was only by petitioning the manorial lord, Thomas Halsall that Kirkby's practices were curtailed.

When the encounter with the manorial lord Thomas Halsall occurred it became more than a civil matter, it became a clash of personalities and personal grievances. Kirkby was taken before the assizes at Preston and accused on several accounts of extorting money from villagers, of using seditious and erroneous language and of taking parts of the tithes which the rector had leased. It also went against him that he had no dwelling but took boarding at various places and frequently in the tavern where he ate all his meals.

Kirkby brought counter charges against Thomas Halsall accusing him of threatening to have him forcibly removed from the altar if he said mass. He also accused him of attempted murder, saying that the lord once made one of his servants lie in wait to kill the curate. On another occasion he alleged that Thomas Halsall sent seventeen men in a gang to the house of William Prescot, where he was at table, with orders to drive him out of the house or else kill him; they actually drove him into the next parish and forbade him to return. In the middle of the following night some of the same men came to the house of Gilbert Kirkby (the curate's father) in Aughton, opened the window of the priest's room with a dagger, and with 'a coal of fire' kindled a 'burden' of straw, intending to burn him to death. Fortunately he had remained awake and so he escaped.

(This is detailed in the Duchy of Lancaster, Pleadings (n. d.), xxi, K5.)

We do not know the judicial outcome of this feud as the records are lost. However, there is no record of Kirkby in Halsall again and it is unlikely that he would have returned to the village. We can only speculate that the church redeployed him to victimise another parish.

Halsall Church in the 17th and 18th Centuries

The 17th and 18th centuries are almost a dark age as far as the history of Halsall Church is concerned and we know relatively little about St Cuthbert's during this time. It was a period where the church fabric was run down and it was in need of much repair and renovation.

In the previous century much change had occurred throughout the realm due to the Reformation, which curtailed medieval Catholic practices and resulted in physical change to the church. Our knowledge after the end of the reign of Elizabeth I in 1603 is scant. We can presume that despite a reluctance to change church services, the Book of Common Prayer services were becoming established. This was to change with the onset of the Civil War and the siege of Lathom House by Cromwellian forces. Ormskirk was bombarded with canon from Clieves Hill to the east of Halsall and Puritan soldiers are reputed to have billeted in Halsall Church. Cromwell's Puritan soldiers were under orders to destroy any Catholic imagery or Icons that remained in parish churches. Graffiti on the tombs of Edward Halsall and his lady dates from this time though damage elsewhere seems superficial. It is alleged that the noses were hacked off the saints on the sedilla in the chancel. It may be also that medieval stained glass was smashed beyond repair. To the right of the altar new stone inserts suggest that a statue matching the one that remains of St Cuthbert, may have stood in a crocketed recess but that this was destroyed. What is unclear is whether this happened during the Reformation purges or was carried out later on by the Puritans. It could be, however, that the soldiers here in Halsall, had to behave with restraint because they were wary of the local feeling. The villagers were still dragging their feet about the Reformation and were barely tolerant of a Puritan regime. After all the soldiers depended on the locals to feed them and provide them with fuel and shelter while they were billeted in the village.

While the Reformation had banned certain Catholic traditions, the Commission set up under the Commonwealth (Puritan) regime passed ordinances that banned The Book of Common Prayer, and rituals prescribed therein. It banned candles and crucifixes, vestments, screens and fonts. Halsall has two ancient Baptismal fonts and neither was destroyed, suggesting that Halsall was not conformable to Puritan pressure. There was a restriction put on the church feasts and even the institutions of birth, marriage and death came under new curbs. This had the effect of discouraging people from attending church because they were unable to participate in a traditional way. The restoration of the monarchy under Charles II brought the gentry back to church but only gradually did the people return. At first they followed the gentry's lead but at a price. A hierarchy of position became manifest when pews were installed. This meant division and deference within the church building with the rich having the finer pews nearer the front and the poor having kneelers at the back.

The gentry dominated space within the church, the walls were filled with military plaques and memorabilia. Now the leading tenant farmers had responsibility for the church as Churchwardens. It was the time of the prosperous Incumbent with glebe and tithe, someone between a parson and a squire. In the opening decades of the 19th century complacency was commonplace, the poor curate taking on ever more duties for a pittance while the congregation were not stimulated by a passive clergy

In Halsall the church school was built in 1695 and the 18th century saw a period when the Church of England was a bedrock of the state. It was an age of patriotism and much of the military ornament and furnishing was installed in the church in the 18th and 19th centuries of Empire. There was, during the late 18th century, a consolidation of church and state.

The onset of Empire and the growth of urbanisation left the Church of England out of touch with the rural parishioners. By the year 1873 the church was badly in need of refurbishment. The floor level was altered and some gravestones were taken out of the chancel and placed between the porch and the grammar school. A church organ was installed and the stonework restored in places where it was crumbling. The Victorians revitalised a decaying church bringing restoration, congregational singing of hymns and improved attendances.

Halsall church is a medieval church with a great stamp of Victoriana on it.

Halsall, a Catholic History

Halsall is situated in south west Lancashire between Ormskirk and Sefton and neighbouring Scarisbrick and Downholland. It has in the past, included all of Downholland and Melling and Altcar as part of its ecclesiastical area. Lancashire is well known for having been the heartland of resistance to the Reformation and clinging on to the 'Old Faith Catholicism'. Indeed at the time of the Reformation, Lancashire was the most Catholic county in England and recent research suggests that Catholicism continued to flourish in Lancashire in spite of the Reformation. Over the next three hundred years from the 16th to the 19th centuries the church and community in Halsall was to be influenced very slowly by the changes in religion nationally, due mainly to local practices and allegiances.

The local church started in 1320 was a typical Catholic church serving the area as far south as Lydiate and across to Ainsdale and Formby. It was so constructed as to contain, four chapels in all, each with a piscina that stored holy water for blessing. The Easter sepulchre, which houses the tomb of Richard Halsall, (the Rector throughout the turbulent time of the Reformation) was an area of special devotion and would be dressed at Eastertide with flowers and images especially for the occasion. The rood loft and clerestory window are reminders of the Catholic ritual and practice whereby passion plays would be enacted on the rood screen. This magnificently carved wooden structure was at some time dismantled and destroyed after the Reformation. The columns still show the scars of the great hinges which would have secured this great screen. The still visible and audible sanctuary bell cote rang the angelus across the fields where farm workers and villagers stopped and recited the prayer to the virgin at midday and at six o'clock eventide.

The official survey of recusancy in the province of York 1596 showed that Halsall had 8 recusants, that is 8 members of well to do families paying for the privilege of continuing to practise their Catholic faith. Despite the Reformation and the harsh laws that drove Catholicism underground during Elizabeth's reign, the old faith still persisted and was slow to change. Many people followed the example set by the great families around the area who clung on to their faith against all resistance. Thus the Blundells of Crosby, the Irelands, the Scarisbricks, Gorsuch and Halsalls were but the tip of an iceberg in a Lancashire which remained devout and loyal to Catholicism. Many of these families sent sons to France to be trained as priests and they returned to Lancashire to perpetuate Catholicism. James Gorsuch was from Gorsuch Hall on the boundary between Halsall and Scarisbrick he studied at Douai in France and returned as a priest in 1705. By the end of the 16th century Catholicism's troubles were only just starting; the next century would see the harsher penalties brought in under the reign of Edward VI and the Puritan zeal leading to greater sanctions against Catholics. Then at the end of the 17th century, William of Orange would arrive epitomizing an antipathy of Catholicism that has persisted in some quarters to the present day.

How did Halsall fare in all this upheaval? First the church may have retained outward appearances of Catholicism much as Sefton church still does to this day. It may have retained its rood screen and loft for performance of the mystery plays until quite late after the reforms, but the church would have had to conform albeit in outward appearance under Edward VI's reign. It was largely however the patron and his appointed rector who would dictate the rate of change or lack of it. The people in an agrarian way of life were slow and reluctant to change centuries of practice. Queen Mary's reign in 1553 attempted to reinstate all the Catholic ways and even after her death, Elizabeth's early years on the throne seemed uncertain and precarious. The reformation of the people was to be a long drawn out process and the Catholic flame would not be snuffed out in Halsall and certainly not in Lancashire.

A picture of Lancashire Catholic gentry households in 1639 shows 4 in Halsall and Altcar as against only 3 in Sefton. Well after Elizabeth had gone we see Catholic resistance becoming more militant. The gunpowder plot under James I and the wave of anti-Catholic feeling it provoked meant Catholics had to tread more warily under charges of being a subversive sect. In Lancashire especially recusants were viewed with much suspicion. During the Civil war between Cromwell's Parliamentarians and the Cavaliers loyal to Charles I, Catholics supported the King who had Catholic sympathies and thus we find Nicholas Blundell of Crosby bearing arms and being wounded for the cause in 1642. The next year his house was searched by Roundheads. Such actions against Catholics and the harsh penal laws would have suggested a compliance of the people of Halsall and this may well have been the outward display but when we go on a hundred years hence to the reign of George III a House of Lords census of all papists in every parish shows 228 in Halsall, 146 in Aughton and 757 in Sefton in 1767.

We know that the Halsall family incumbents of the local church, Richard and Cuthbert 1513-1563 and1563-1571 respectively were Catholic and their successor George Hesketh also preferred the old faith. The Halsall's kept the position of Rector under their patronage until 1633. This was well into the reign of Charles I. The patronage during the Elizabethan era 1558-1603 was under Edward Halsall the squire who was considered 'conformable (to the Protestant religion) but of no good note'. By this it was meant that inwardly he did not conform, he was a 'recusant' and he swore to die 'a good Catholic'. Cuthbert, his successor as squire, also kept the incumbency of the church in the family and he was very much of the old faith. He suffered hardship financially for this allegiance under penal laws but he brought up his sons to fight for the King against Cromwellian forces in the civil war.

So perhaps we can come to understand why, when the census of papists in 1767 showed 228 Catholics, there were so many in the parish who remained 'unreformed'. The squires and rectors had been very uncommitted to the reformers cause and the people tended to follow the example of their masters. The Halsall family rectors presided from 1495-1594 this only being broken by George Hesketh who in the full throes of Elizabeth's reign was a devout Catholic. After Hesketh came Peter Travers, who was frequently absent, but a royalist: he was fervently against the Puritanical excesses of Protestantism. He was followed by Nathaniel Jackson briefly before Thomas Johnson, a Presbyterian for 15 years. Then came another Rector 'more absent than not' in Mathew Smallwood who was occupied with other charges in Gawsworth and Lichfield. Halsall was not getting the earnest Protestant reformers to which much of the country had succumbed but rather it experienced gradual piecemeal change in Rectors who failed to insist on conformity to the reformed ways.

Certainly new lawful edicts were enforced and so the rood screen would have been taken down and probably burnt. The many niches which would have held statues of the saints are now mostly empty including the St

A rood screen and rood loft

Nicholas niche on the most western corner of the tower. Possibly the church walls were covered in medieval paintings and these would have been whitewashed away; but such barbarous acts of vandalism were commonplace under Henry VIII and his descendants. There is no evidence of structural damage the kind wrought by a mob whipped up into a frenzy by anti-Catholic propaganda. The piscinas and sedilla remain intact, the fabric largely undamaged by the enforced changes, suggesting a gradual and reluctant conformity.

It was Smallwood's curate, Nathaniel Brownwell who probably effected most change by getting involved with the community and school and restoring the building of the church which had fallen into some neglect. His patron was the Earl of Macclesfield and he held office for 35 years. His term of office covered the time of the so called 'Glorious Revolution' under William of Orange when anti-Catholic feeling ran high and penal laws were enacted. He stood up on the Sunday morning of the 16th September 1683 and upheld the 39 Articles of Faith of the Protestant religion. The successor to Brownwell was Albert le Blanc who was French by birth and not a protestant reformer or zealot in any way; neither was David Cromarque who was incumbent until 1746. The advent of the Mordaunt's as patrons in the latter half of the 18th century was the first lasting association with what we envisage the Church of England to be today. At this time over 200 of Halsall's population were still Roman Catholics which suggests that the pace of religious change was neither a reformation or revolution in Halsall.

Religion in Halsall after the Reformation

It is well documented that Lancashire remained the most Catholic county in England in the late Tudor period and that the north western sea board was the least touched by Protestant reformers. This may have had something to do with the inaccessibility of the region and the strong devotion of the local gentry families to the Catholic faith. Nevertheless, there were communities like Little Crosby and Altcar which up to the reign of Charles II claimed that they had not a reformer or Protestant in their village. The feudal deference in the agricultural landscape of medieval England persisted in Lancashire well into the middle of the 16th century. Halsall was a backwater village and a close knit agricultural community. Its position was determined geographically by being surrounded by marsh to the west and north. Only Ormskirk to the east offered a market and access to other important trading centres. The Lord of the Manor was powerful and his word often determined the patronage of the church and he chose the Rector. He also applied the law locally and how the law would be interpreted in accordance with local customs.

Pressure on Catholics was severe in the reign of Edward VI and during most of Elizabeth's reign. The Penal Laws imposed fines for being 'non conformable' and this meant varying sanctions on Catholics, according to the political situation. It was at times so stringent that Catholicism would not have survived without the help of sympathetic Protestants in local power. Thus the burial of 'Papists' was still permitted in the churchyard, (Papist was a derogatory term meaning those still loyal to the Pope) Some of the new laws were petty and unenforceable. The banning of beads for prayer was a curb on tradition steeped in the ritual of the calendar of feasts which governed the rural year. Prayers accompanied the beating of the bounds, the sowing, the weeding, the harvesting and the threshing. It was very hard for customs like these to be just stopped. The move against images and icons lead to many people taking these objects and hiding them in their homes rather than see them sequestrated by the King's men. After all, these items in the church were often paid for by the villagers and a sense of communal ownership prevailed.

As most Catholics were tenant farmers or farm labourers they had little in the way of possession and therefore little means to pay fines and penalties. Undoubtedly the new ways of the Reformers had adherents, but they were not zealous and there is no great evidence of the smashing of images as required under Edward's Act of 1549. Apart from one holy water stoop being defaced and the noses knocked off images on the sedilla in the chancel, little other damage was enacted.* There was a hand staying any excess of this sort and it was deference to the way of life of the old religion and the Manorial Lord who guarded the status quo. There existed therefore a leniency which was the product of confusion and uncertainty by the law enforcers. They hesitated until the heavy hand of a visitation of the King's Commissioners made enacting penalties inevitable, for crimes of which they were unconvinced.

With the death of Edward VI in 1553 and the accession of Mary I the images were brought out of hiding and the old ways restored. Mary was a Catholic and wanted the reforms turned back and Catholicism reinstated. For the ordinary people of these shores a collective sigh of relief ensured that normal service would be resumed as soon as possible. Under Mary, the Sarum Rite of the mass reappeared, images, lights, bells, pilgrimages, wall paintings, beads, processions and feast days were all resumed. However this was only partly achieved as change was slow and funding had not recovered.

When Mary died some 6 years later, her half sister Elizabeth came to the throne as the champion of reforming protestant ways.

It is little wonder that the ordinary men and women of the realm had a sceptical outlook to the re emergence of new reforms. The new queen was a mere girl on a tottering throne. Everyone knew that the Duke of Norfolk was the most powerful man in England and he a Catholic. The proximity of Spanish empire made the situation for the queen and the Protestant reformers even more precarious. Small wonder then that parishes like Halsall, set in the midst of Catholic Lancashire, clinging vehemently to traditional ways, decided they would wait until reform came to them rather than actively pursue it. The Bishop of Chester was ineffective at ensuring change and so lip service was paid to visitations from the Church Commissioners and Halsall dragged its feet. The Halsall folk did not want to be bullied into a way of living which felt uncomfortable and wrong. If reform must come, better it were embraced by the next generation

While images were proscribed, the ritual of the agrarian calendar meant the rhythms of offerings and blessings, bells and smells continued despite changes in décor. The changes that hit hardest was the the physical change to the fabric. The dismantling of the rood screen, the abandoning of the Easter sepulchre, the whitewashing of wall paintings, the removal of candlelight and removal of images like the doom painting above the chancel arch, had to be accepted. However, in the people's hearts the old devotions were still practised and cherished.

The church seemed much more dreary and uninviting. Much grumbling and reluctance created a mood of discontent. It was only changes over a generation which would bring eventually acceptance of Lutheran reforms, but for now in each and every small way ritual was adhered to and customs were practised covertly if not openly. When the church was locked on Easter eve, by order of the Bishop, preventing the centuries old practice of vigil over the Easter sepulchre, villagers gathered outside with candles as near to the sepulchre as physically possible, sometimes staying through the night. Increasingly people saw themselves as locked out of Heaven. With the loss of the Rood screen the physical separation between the sacred part of the church, the chancel and the secular part ,the nave, was broken. Now the whole church became solemn. Activities which were somewhat hidden by the screen such as ale brewing, livestock markets, dancing and gossiping were now exposed before the altar of Almighty God. The loss of this space meant the loss of activity and less social cohesion. In the same way that the old religion was driven underground so the social activities usually conducted in the nave went outside and away from the central point of the village.

However the rural way of life insisted that old rituals like blessing the fields continued for fear that the harvest would fail. Livelihoods depended on it so no edict from London was going to change things fast. An agricultural village like Halsall couldn't take the risk of a bad harvest, so the church rituals in time and harmony with the countryside would go on. 'Any road up' the Halsall folk had enough to mutter and moan about with the abrogation of feast days. It was more work and less leisure, rest and devotion and seemed a 'bad bargain' for country folk where life was hard enough and the seasons unforgiving. So it was that reform took on the gradual pace of generational change which would eventually bring acceptance. As the old generation died out so the next generation might be more conformable. Gradually then Halsall came into line with new laws though all around resistance continued.

Indeed it is debateable if this damage wasn't sustained 100 years later when Cromwell's troops were billeted in the church. This was the occasion when they pounded Ormskirk with cannonball prior to the siege of Lathom Hall 1644.

SECTION II

CHRISTMAS AT HALSALL
THROUGH THE AGES

Christmas 1349 The Black Death

Of all the Christmastides celebrated in Halsall and England, none can have been so sad and solemn as the Christmas of 1349. Not even when Cromwell banned Christmas in the mid 1600's or the dark days of 1940/41 when the Nazis threatened, could there have been less cheer at the church and in the quiet lanes of Halsall parish.

The angelus bell, which marked the turning of the hours, was silent for the few workers who gathered the neglected winter root crops for the festive table that year. The winter ale had not been freshly brewed and last year's stale brew slid down throats a bitter cup after the year's events. The barest decoration festooned the church. A bit of holly and ivy and a tallow candle here and there. The bees had gone from the bee garden so carefully tended for decades. The bee keepers had been slain and no smell of fine beeswax for the Christmastide was to be had.

It was a year which at the start had promised so much. Good harvests of arable crops had been sold at Ormskirk's flourishing market. The population in the village had grown in number with more land workers setting up home and the work on the new church was progressing. The old Norman church which had been mainly wooden in structure, had been levelled in 1320 to allow the building of the new church from finest sandstone. This had come to pass because the old church could not cope with the growing congregation and there had been much optimism hope and pride in local achievement with the construction of the new church but this had now come to a grinding halt. When the master mason fell ill it was a sore day for Halsall. He had been one of the first to die and had his funeral in amongst the construction where he had plied his skills. His coffin swayed from side to side on the cart as it splashed through ruts and pot holes on its way to church in that cold and miserable spring of 1349.

The villagers had been forewarned. Travellers brought the first tales of a plague sweeping across Europe from the East. It had hit Rome in autumn 1348 and by the time it swept to the foreign ports just across the channel, the Rector Milngate foretold, from the pulpit, news of a terrible pestilence. He emphasized the need for contrition which would require the parishioners to engage in much penitential praying, fasting and ritual to appeal to God to spare his blessed congregation. At the start of the new year 1349 the plague was rife in London. By the middle of May the first cases of this new plague were reported in Ormskirk and terror filled the homes of Halsall folk. The plague scythed through the land taking with it half the population. Death usually occurred within a few days of the first symptoms, which were coughing up blood, huge abscesses and lungs filled with fluid and meant death was imminent. It was highly contagious and hit all manner of men, women and children not differentiating between rich and poor, good and bad, healthy and weak. It was the bubonic plague or Black Death. The churchwardens succumbed to the pestilence as did the curate. Work was stopped on the rebuilding of the church because half the labourers had died and the number of masons diminished. Many valuable artisan skills were lost to the sickness. Reverend Milngate could scarcely get an altar server and the Sanctus bell fell silent. In the fields the crops of wheat and barley were ragged with weeds. Animals fell ill for want of attention. The heavy rains during the harvest made matters worse hampering the efforts of the few who were able to gather in the harvest. Stray animals wandering over the crops caused damage as fences were left unrepaired and animals untended.

The building work on the church stopped and for several months the churchyard took on an unattractive appearance with mounds of earth indicating foundations waiting to be laid and others pits where the dead were recently interred. The churchyard was quickly filled and bones from older graves were collected and housed in an ossuary near and beneath the present high altar where they remain to this day. It may well have been that graves were dug outside of consecrated ground and soon all the land about and around the church was churned up with new graves.

Christmas 1349 was an occasion to mark the passing of the year and the loss of many loved family and friends. With the pestilence cleared by October the drift back to church had been slow and hesitant. Advent and Christmas was the time for new beginnings. Some labourers had found that their work was able to command higher wages and the local taverns did a brisk trade but generally in a farming community the shortage of labour led to problems.

It was the aftermath of the Black Death which eventually led to some prosperity for Halsall. While the price of other arable crops failed wheat prices remained high and Halsall, with its large flat fields, was able to sustain wheat production albeit on a smaller scale because of labour shortage. With Halsall being remote and surrounded by marshland, outside influences were fewer and the locals may well have honoured their fealty to their lords of the manor, the Halsalls and maybe did not exploit their bargaining power to the extent which had happened in other parts of the realm. There was a change in farming from some arable to livestock involving more sheep and strains of sheep which were less susceptible to foot rot on the marshland around Halsall. Wool was to become lucrative in the latter part of the 14th century and the prosperity of Halsall, with a mixed concentration on arable and livestock, grew to the point where the construction of the church could continue and the fine chancel started in 1340 could be finished in 1370: which in its grandeur was considered one of the best in England.

Within the Chancel high up on the apex of the eastern window is a carving of a hand raised in benediction. It seems to signify that God's hand has blessed and spared the congregation after the great plague had taken so many. It is a reminder of God's mercy to his cherished survivors and also that the hand raised in benevolence could easily strike them down if they sin. On the outside of the chancel the seven deadly sins were carved in grotesque form, which hang there today, ravaged by the weather of 7 centuries but still a reminder of the consequences of sin. Certainly the splendour of the chancel was intended for the nave also but work seems to have stopped for some 60 years until 1430 when an octagonal tower was added to the church and it took more or less the shape we have today. The plague however was to return but never with the severity of the year 1349.

Halsall Christmastide 1547

Snowy Morning

These have been strange times since the old king Henry VIII died in January of this year. There has been a lot made of these reforming ideas from the continent and the old king's dissatisfaction with the Pope. So many changes we have seen here at Halsall during his reign, many pronouncements, many edicts, some we have had to act on and some we have just not bothered with. The worst one for me was the Act for the abrogation of holidays; this was 11 years since but is only just being put into practice these last few years here in Lancashire. This act puts a curb on the many saint's days that give us rest and an excuse to make merry. We have lost many feast days including St Thomas a Becket, Mary Magdelene and our own St Cuthbert. We used to celebrate his feast day on September 4th as well as the anniversary of his death on March 20th. This first date was to commemorate his remains being taken from the Holy island at Lindisfarne to Durham Cathedral. It is 10 years since King Henry's commissioners destroyed his shrine at Durham and found his body uncorrupted. Anyway, although the holy days are fewer, I suppose we have more days for earning wages.

Richard Halsall is the incumbent at the church and he is very set in his ways, he hasn't the mind for many of these new fangled reforms. Other churches in this area have tarried over changes to their churches but I have heard it said that in the south of the realm the reforms have been carried through to the letter. We became part of the new diocese of Chester six years since, but we have scarcely had a visit from the Bishop John Bird and we have secured his wrath by being tardy and non compliant with the new orders. However some of the old ways have gone gradually. We're not allowed to ring the angelus bells now, so when we are labouring in the fields we never know our break times. Someone has scratched a dial against the side of the church wall but it's so often cloudy we take a guess at the position of the sun in the sky. Lucky for us, the closing down of the priory at Burscough in 1536 has meant we have just gained possession of some new choir benches for our lovely new chancel. They have beautiful carvings on and under there are misericords, these are elaborate little seats which afforded the monks some rest when they stood during long services. There is one carving of wrestlers. I have heard only Ely Cathedral has such a similar carving.

We still have the Rogation processions in April, but it is said 'we are charming the fields' and it is frowned upon. The Easter devotions are not as elaborate as they used to be and now the changes are affecting Christmas this year. I looked forward to the run up to Christmas starting with Michelmas on 29th September and then 40 days later Martinmas on November 11th. These were great days of festivity and a chance to get together with neighbours and friends. It was also a time to plan ahead for Christmas itself, which was a revelry that sometimes went on to Candlemas on February 2nd. Now all the revelry and devotion on those saints' days is forbidden under the new boy king Edward VI. A royal decree this year has stated that the clergy and the people are to take away and destroy all shrines, candlesticks, paintings, chalices, veils and vestments. Walls are to be whitewashed and stained glass windows broken. Archbishop Cranmer at Canterbury is working on a new prayer book to be used in all churches in two years time.

At least we still have Christmas. The holiday is not as long as it usually was, but we are ahead with brewing the ale in the church nave for Christmas Eve. I expect if they ever take down the big Rood screen, which separates the chancel from the nave, we will not be allowed to bring our animals into the nave and barter to haggle over prices, or to brew ales and hold festivities in church. It won't seem right with the Altar exposed we'll have to be reverential all the time. We will have lost our community meeting point. We aren't allowed to light as many candles in front of our favourite statues and the church looks a lot duller for it. In the same way there aren't as many bouquets brought into the church. I don't suppose there will be any plays allowed this year, it doesn't bode well. Time was there was lovely singing at Christmas, plainchant from the monks at Burscough priory and carols in the nave on Christmas Eve. Now it's much bleaker and subdued. I bet they will ban Christmas itself in the not too distant future. Aye it's queer times alright.

John Cowper, farm labourer November 1547
(fictional character and account based on historical fact)

The Christmas tale of Claviger 1548

Claviger was a watcher. He had been in the service of Halsall's manorial lords since birth; he was the runt of a family of 7 boys and 2 girls. His stature tended towards slight, and his swarthy sallow complexion did not endear him to people. His eyes were cold and never seemed completely open but they saw everything and his ears were alert to all gossip. Most of his time was spent tending his masters' dogs in the stables, where he lived amongst the horses and the hay. On Sundays and holy days Claviger had the important responsibility of being a key holder; he opened the church in the morning and shut it again in the night. His key also opened the little door in the St Nicholas chantry chapel, which led to the winding steps over the chancel arch. At the top in the turret he crouched and watched through squints in the stone work which gave onto the churchyard, the nave and the altar. His task was to watch for wrong doing, to listen for any scrap of conversation which might be of interest and which he could relay back to the rector and the patron his master. Henry Halsall, the patron and lord of Halsall manor impressed on him that his role was vital. The manor and the church needed to know what the people were saying, this was how order was maintained and transgressors brought to book. But Claviger was zealous in his task. He was wont to embellishment of these actions he perceived and tittle-tattle he overheard and the villagers despised him as an informer. Claviger was as nimble as he was devious. If he did not want people to know if he was in his turret, he would climb up the stonework and enter the turret from the parapet on the roof. It was better for him to observe who was late for mass, hurrying across the churchyard after the gospel bell. He watched for lapses in concentration during the consecration of the Eucharist. He saw irreverence in whispers, in muffled laughter, for those who failed to kneel when the host was held high, or those who failed to strike their breast in contrition. All was reported back, he was meticulous with detail. His efforts were rewarded with a small coin tossed to the floor by the curate, for which Claviger scraped on all fours in the dust.

Out in the village, Claviger was treated with suspicion and shunned, save for two shepherds, who bided their time drinking a gill with him and listening to his tales of gossip in the White Horse tavern. "That one Alice who lives next to the Smithy gives herself airs and graces, I've seen her flirting in the church with looks and curtsies to young yeomen but she has a mouth like a midden when she's driving the geese from her vegetable garden. The curate is no better, he's fond of the communion wine when the rector's back is turned." When folk in the village stopped to talk, they first looked around to make sure Claviger wasn't lurking behind a wall or in the undergrowth. He brought unease and he operated under his lordship's protection.

At Christmastide the mummers arrived. They were a theatrical travelling group who performed plays of mystery relating events in Christ's life but also they did comedy. They often mimicked Claviger to the delight of their audience. Their spectacle was performed on the rood loft, which was a platform above the rood screen in the church. The audience watched from the nave below, the antics of the mummers above. This rood screen covered the whole of the chancel arch and therefore the access to it was by ascending the narrow winding stairs, where Claviger kept watch in his turret. The mummers entered onto the rood loft through the little door high up above the enclosed pulpit. They pushed past him in his turret perch on their way to perform mystery plays on the rood loft. They chided him, "You are a despicable fellow Claviger, you spy like Judas." "You are neglecting your dogs they skulk around like you do after your master." "You should stay in mime and not open your mouths," retorted Claviger receiving a painful prod from St

George's sword, courtesy of the last mummer. Claviger winced, he hated the mummers. They came every year and every year he spitefully kept them waiting in the cold for the church to be opened. One year the mummers stuffed all the yuletide holly in the turret causing Claviger a very uncomfortable time as he tried to perform his 'watching.'

The Hidden Gargoyle, Claviger?

It was after the death of King Henry in 1547 that laws were passed under the boy king Edward VI banning mystery plays. The mummers found their repertoire curtailed and so spent more time on comedy, mimicking Claviger became a main theme of their entertainment. Claviger decided he would sort out these mummers once and for all. He went out on the moss one cold December morn to cut himself a cudgel from a gnarled old bog oak growing in the marsh. Hurrying back before daybreak he fell in the marsh and caught a very bad fever. For two weeks Claviger was scarcely able to lift himself from slumber except to take a bit of pottage brought by the other servants. It was during these two weeks that under the reforms, the great rood screen and loft were removed onto the churchyard where the villager, dismantled it and took the fine wood into their homes, lest the commissioners burn the structure. The mummers, when they came just before Christmas, had no rood loft to perform on but they put together a makeshift platform in the nave and began their routine. The play was in session when Claviger decided he had enough strength to return to the church. Concealing his cudgel he scampered up onto the parapet on the outside of the church and into his turret hide out. On hearing the taunts of the mummers he brandished his cudgel and jumped through the rood loft door!

Claviger's blood seeped from a broken skull in his fall from the chancel arch. He had silenced the mummers.

Halsall Christmas 1789 (Year of Floods, Revolution and Mutiny)

This passing year 2007 has seen the worst floods in England since 1789. Rain fell incessantly throughout June and July. Tewkesbury was cut off and surrounded by water, while its famous abbey was isolated on an island and the floods entered the chapter house. Halsall Church like Tewkesbury Abbey is built on an outcrop making it higher than the surrounding area. This gives a prominence to the church and makes its spire look higher and visible over many miles, it also permits the safety of secure ground. We were luckier in this area though crops were ruined.

The situation was very different however 200 years ago and dry ground was a very important issue in a marshland area during the year of floods. In 1760 Edward Segar of Barton House, who had been church warden from 1729- 1737, started to reclaim land by a long process of drain building and surface stripping and burning. This was bearing some success, for more farms were becoming established. The canal had been started at Halsall in 1770 and was by 1789 navigable on a good stretch down to Liverpool. Prosperity then was coming to this area but only slowly. This prosperity was tempered however by appalling weather. In these years harsh winters meant the Thames froze over and frost fairs were held on the ice. The very wet weather of 1789 came after and probably in response to an exceptionally dry year in 1788. Glover Moore was the Rector having been made so in 1778. He inherited a church in a state of decay and disrepair. The north aisle and vestry suffered the most from leaks and damp in the badly decayed stonework. It was the reign of George III and church attendance had fallen. The increase in farming and communication was slow to translate into income for the church coffers and no attempt to refurbish the church would be made for another 30 years. The walls were crumbling; the roof leaked in several places and the floor in the nave was uneven and damp.

The Church of England had travailed through the upheaval of the Reformation and the tribulations of the Civil War which brought a Commonwealth and it was only now that the Church of England began to settle as the established church in England. This was an age of divine right, passive obedience and non resistance. With the Mordaunts as patrons this stability was at long last taking a hold at St Cuthbert's. 1789 however, brought a prevailing sense of fear about revolution. It was the year of the storming of the Bastille in Paris setting a train of events which would lead to France being declared a republic. In Britain the Admiralty was rocked by Fletcher Christian and the mutineers who had set Captain Bligh adrift from his ship the Bounty. Authority and establishment seemed to be threatened. An artist Thomas Turner made a painting of the interior of the church depicting one of Glover Moore's sermons. It was possibly used as a cover for the London Illustrated News. The suggestion is that Glover Moore was preaching a sermon on the Napoleonic wars. A hanging of the King's coat of Arms can be seen prominent above the chancel arch. The aspect is one of gloom and a sparse but the very conservatively dressed congregation appear weary of the sermon and its message.

Little really is known about our church and it's congregation in the 18th century. It is with some imagination that we can envisage a cold damp Church that greeted the worshippers who congregated that Christmas morn 1789. Some had come by carriage spattered with mud on the rut filled lanes, others may have crossed the marshes and tethered small boats not far from the church; some arrived on foot crossing the new canal bridges and cobbled lanes. The mood this Christmas was more sombre than joyous. The patron had upset the local farmers by insisting on a tithe on potatoes. The church needed the money for repairs. Glover Moore was 54 in this year and would preside for another 19 years. The Mordaunt's, notes Cotterall in his book on Halsall, had started a small cotton industry and the brook was dammed across the road from the church to provide power for the machinery. There was however some dispute over patents with Richard Arkwright and this would eventually lead to the Mordaunts terminating Halsall's brief flirtation with the Industrial Revolution and subsequently losing the patronage of the church by selling it to the Blundells. This would eventually prove beneficial for the fabric of the church but at the end of the 18th century the former merriment of medieval Christmas seemed a long way away.

Church viewed from Mordaunt's mill.

Christmas 1997, The light of the Universe

I recall Christmas eve 1997 when a storm accompanied by very strong southerly winds brought down power lines and consequently all Haskayne, Barton and Halsall on the west side of the canal bridge were without power. It meant many a turkey remained uncooked until the following day and candles were brought out a plenty in houses and hostelries. It was all very inconvenient on this important night of family festivity, but for those who attended the midnight service at the parish church it was like walking through a time warp back to medieval times. The service was lit by candlelight and there was no heating. The organ could not work but there was piano accompaniment to the carols, the only concession to Modern times. The celebration of Communion at midnight appeared as it would have done for centuries There are not words which can describe the simple beauty of the church that night, nor describe the affinity which those, who were lucky enough to be present, felt with our ancestors of old who for centuries experienced the cold winter darkness pierced only by natural flame. They would have made their way home by moonlight or starlight, weather permitting and had none of the frippery that we attach to Christmas. The teaching of a Saviour, come as a light into the world would carry so much more significance. We were given an individual candle to read the service by. In former times this would have been an extravagance allowed only for special occasions. The liturgy in medieval times would have been in Latin and known by heart and learnt by rote. Even when the service was conducted in English there were probably few who could read or see their Book of Common Prayer to respond by candle light.

On Advent evening our service often starts in darkness; until the great hymn 'O Come Emmanuel'. We get a few moments when the church is in darkness and then the light is brought in. We exit the church at the end of the service and rarely see the stars in their magnificence because of light pollution from streetlights, from security lights and from the pall of sky glow. Even our Christmas lights, as pretty as they are, can not be seen to full effect unless in a darkened location. They too are swamped by pervading light from other sources. Starlight, which was so significant to our ancestors is forgotten and ignored in the colourful razzmatazz of Christmas. We cannot see the light for the lights! Is this not the problem with Christmas today? We lose the real natural light and replace it with artificial light. We can look at the most beautiful Christmas lights and admire but they will never induce the wonderment and awe which the Universe and He who made it inspire

Christmas 2012 (Claviger's release)

A soft rain had dampened the stone under which the body of Claviger lay. Claviger was a nickname derived from the French for 'key holder' because he had the keys to the church. One of his jobs had been to say chantry prayers for the dead in the Chantry chapel of St Nicholas to the right of the main altar in St Cuthbert's. This he had done faithfully until he died in 1546, but there had been no one to say prayers for him for over 450 years. His burial stone had been hidden by means of turves which had grown over his plot but recently it had been uncovered during a tidy up by parishioners. On Christmas Eve the Christmas tree, erected annually in the churchyard, was bedecked with lights and they reflected off the smooth surface of the 16th century stone. Curiously this had coincided with the due date of Claviger's release from the torment of purgatory and into peace and forgiveness. It was the believed in 16th century Europe that when a person died, their soul atoned for wrong doing before passing into Heaven. The very wicked went to Hell. The years had passed quickly and were uninterrupted, the inscription on the church clock said it all. "Praetereunt Imputantur". He had lived his hours and been held to account for them.

However there remained one problem; to return to your family meant being remembered and when that happened the Christmas candle, lit in the bosom of your family at Christmas dinner, was also lit for you. This was carried like a beacon through generations so that your descendants reached forgotten souls. The Christmas candle cut through centuries of shadow. In this way the spirits could all gather at the Christmas table and be part of the celebration of the birth of Christ. Claviger, however, had no one. It would take some significant recognition to release him from his limbo at Christmastide. What chance had he? He was forgotten for nearly 500 years covered under sods of earth without an inscription on his slab.

At the Christmas midnight service, the visiting priest started his sermon and one drowsy little boy James Spence wanted an end to it. He was bored. The midnight service wasn't like the Christingle, where Paul the Rector had excited all the children to a fever pitch of expectation. This was just carols and prayers. He picked up his dad's car keys and played with them turning an imaginary lock. He was from a family which stretched back generations in Halsall, but no one in his family had ever done the family research. He yawned and glanced at the board which contained all the rectors stretching back to 1106 and read down the list until with surprise he came to his own name, James Spence and after it the inscription "alias Claviger!" "Dad look, what does alias mean?" His Dad pondered a moment, a door in another world opened! The next afternoon as the dusk light faded, his mum lit a candle on the Christmas table. They did not know it but they had an extra guest for dinner.

The Rector Board

The Christmas Carol

The outdoor carol service held every year since 2008 is an outstanding success and evokes a spirit of medieval times when carols played a much more important role. Then, of course, there were no brass bands, which are of Victorian origin, but the singing of carols was a traditional way of spreading good cheer and they were sometimes performed by travelling choirs singing at the village cross or in the taverns. This practice continued for many hundreds of years and is wonderfully illustrated in Thomas Hardy's 'Under the Greenwood Tree' which starts with a group of minstrels and singers coming together for the Christmas Eve carol singing in the village of Upper Mellstock.

In medieval times singing in the church grounds was only allowed if permission was given by the incumbent. Singing inside the church during a service was usually only done by the priest, or a trained choir versed in the different offices of service. The church service made provision for sacred chant in Latin at Christmastide but participation by the congregation did not happen. Usually carols were sung in English and were traditional folk songs and therefore not considered solemn enough to be sung in church. The carol as a religious song dates back to the 13th century but it reached its glory days during the 14th century, gaining widespread popularity. The practice was condemned by church councils in 1209 and 1435, because of the similarity to pagan ritual at the solstice. Before carol singing in public became popular, there were sometimes official carol singers called 'Waits'. These were groups of singers led by important local leaders (such as council leaders) who were allowed to beg for alms in this way. They were called 'Waits' because they only sang on Christmas Eve. (This was sometimes known as 'watchnight' or 'waitnight' because the shepherds were watching their sheep when the angels appeared to them.)

When the weather was inclement the villagers would meet in the nave of the church to celebrate festivities. It is conceivable that carols might have been sung at a social gathering in the church but not for or during a service. Over the following hundred years the carol developed musically and as a literary form in its own right and this is largely attributed to the 'lauda,' an Italian religious folk song introduced by the Franciscan monks. This was silenced by the Reformation in England and replaced by the metrical Psalm. Under Cromwell, Christmas was banned from 1647 to 1660, though locals would have sung carols in secret and so they survived. It was the Restoration of Charles II which permitted once again the celebration of Christmas and the singing of carols.

Throughout most of the 18th century in England, the only officially permitted Christmas hymn in church services was 'While Shepherds watched.' Carols such as 'O come all ye faithful', which was written by an English Roman Catholic exile in 1740's, was considered a subversive call to rally the faithful to the Jacobean cause and was banned. A resurgence of carols in the 19th century has helped them become the prerequisite of the Christmas season but almost all the well known carols were not sung in church until the second half of the 19th century. Hymns Ancient and Modern 1861 - 1874 included several carols and most of the popular carols we hear and sing today are of Victorian origin. These carols are often played over and over again in department stores and played in so many different arrangements that they become unrecognizable and just a background noise. There is a wealth of ancient carols lost to our present day conception, great carols such as "O Natus Lux" and "Videte Miraculum" by Thomas Tallis, "Nesciens Mater" by Jean Mouton and 'My Sweet Baby' by William Byrd to name but a few.

In the present day composers such as John Rutter, John Tavener and Morten Lauridsen are creating carols which are sung in the cathedrals along with the great medieval and popular Victorian carols. On the Saturday before Christmas at 3 o'clock in the Anglican Cathedral Liverpool Professor Ian Tracey leads the cathedral choirs in performing all the works which are sung throughout the Christmas period.

Christmas 2013: A Lantern of Light

Floodlit in 1999

Roy Strong in his book on parish churches refers to the medieval parish church as a lantern of light. The perpendicular style of construction opened vast windows of light into the church. Where once they had been cramped dark places, they now resembled the Cathedrals with great expanses of window and fine stonework. The chancel at St Cuthbert's displays these very features. Four huge gothic windows enable, first the rising sun in the east and then on the south side the streams of morning sunlight to enter the altar space and choir. This is never more resplendent than in the winter months when the Sun is low and the sunlight reflects the stained glass on the north wall. A clerestory window was added later and high up on the nave. This lets in further daylight and allowed the rood loft to be lit during passion plays.

While these windows decorated in stain glass let light in, they also had the reverse effect, in the dark part of the year and particularly at Christmas, they enabled the light from within the church to pierce the darkness of a wintery eve.

Presently our church is floodlit and has all manner of electric light inside from spotlights to neon and Led lighting. However one need only go back to the 1950's, when street lighting was new to Halsall and primitive by today's standards, to imagine the darkness surrounding our beautiful church. Yet our church had stood for 600 years before electricity or gas lighting. Then it would have been lit by candles and perhaps at Christmas, by fiery torches. The church with its warm glow and colour would have stood out like a blazing lantern against skies filled with stars crisp and clean on a frosty night unpolluted with artificial light. Consider how the village would have worked together to make this special place even more special at Christmas. Today we have a few volunteers who take pride in sweeping and polishing to maintain the church's comfortable and clean standard. Others devote time to decorate, prepare flowers, Christmas trees and ensure music, light, warmth and a smell of fresh polish. Last Christmas the annual carol event in the churchyard was followed by a candlelight gathering in the Nave. This was the first time for many years that the Nave had been lit by burning flame and was the brainwave of Dave Sephton the churchwarden.

In medieval times, preparing the church for Christmastide would have involved the entire village. The floor would have been re-laid with fresh straw; beeswax would have replaced the smelly tallow of candles. Holly from the churchyard was used to decorate the walls and torches of pitch and oil hung from iron brackets. Church ales were brewed beforehand. In all a very jolly celebration was inclusive of the whole village, to celebrate the birth of a unique baby in Palestine many years ago. And when those medieval worshippers left for home on that sacred night, they would have met total darkness outside. If they were lucky the moon might light their way. Otherwise, after a few moments of adjusting retinas to the dark, the marvellous and miraculous sight of thousands of stars and nebulae would only confirm in their eyes and hearts the wonder and glory of God's creation and power.

Snow Angels (the graveyard in winter)

SECTION III

TALES AND CURIOSITIES

Summer 2008

An Excursion into our Medieval Past

Church warden is never a glamorous occupation, particularly when scraping pigeon droppings from roofs and gullies and repairing leaks to the roof. It was on one such occasion, when accompanying Dave Sephton as an 'aide territoire' that I had the honour and pleasure of delving into our 500+ years' history. As he clambered on the roof over turrets and pinnacles, like a modern day Quasimodo, armed with a bucket and a trowel, my job was to catch him if he slipped off the wet lead. This was to prevent him going headlong over the parapet to the graveyard below; which would have cut out the middle man.

To access the roof of the church it is necessary to enter the small side door of St Nicholas' Chapel in the nave and to climb the narrow stone, turreted stair case up to the Chancel Arch crossing. This was a truly medieval experience. Very little has changed in this stairwell since the church was built in the 14th century. An ornately carved stone newel post begins the ascent up the windy steps. Dave added to the tension by being unable to locate the light switch so we climbed in near darkness through the mustiness and cobwebs of 600 years squatting mostly, as medieval man was of lesser stature than modern man. Halfway up, a small door opens up on to a sheer drop down onto the pulpit. This was the door to the rood loft, the carved wooden platform built on top of the rood screen. It was wide enough to allow the performance of Mystery Plays and other rituals for the congregation below. Both the rood loft and the rood screen disappeared as a result of the Reformation. Further up the windy staircase the smells and textures of 600 years are weathered into the stones which were hewn around the time that the Black Death ravaged the realm. The masons marks abound, signatures of work sculpted to the greater glory of God. The stairs end in a turret on the south side of the Chancel and here the extent of weather erosion on the crocketed spirelets can be viewed with dismay. The elements have taken their toll on the finer detail of the dedicated craftsmen of the past and we may never find again such craftsmen capable of restoring this intricate detail.

At the top of the turret a stepped passageway crosses the Chancel Arch. There are squints which are small look out holes. One squint looks out on the Nave and one onto the Chancel. Here an overseer would watch the congregation while at the same time keeping a check on the progress of the service. He could possibly have been one of the church wardens. At the most solemn moments he would observe that the parishioners were behaving reverently and report back to the Rector and the Patron on nonconforming miscreants. Halfway across this passage is a lever which operates the Sanctus bell, located in the bell cote on the outside pinnacle of the Chancel. It would be rung by the overseer at the moment of consecration and exposition of the Blessed Sacrament. This is also the bell which was rung to signal the Angelus at midday prayers before lunch and at the curfew of the day to signal the end of work in the fields. The bell would originally have been hung within the ornate tower on the roof of the Chancel but now is hung at a lower height letting the sound resound up the cylindrical chamber into the bell cote. The passageway ends in another crocketed turret which looks out onto the churchyard on the north side. The amazing detail viewed from this height is astonishing because few would ever see the work. The bell cote itself is richly decorated with carvings of faces too small to be seen from the ground yet remarkably unweathered over centuries. There were no optical aides then and clambering around on the roof would certainly not have been allowed other than for the masons and a select few. It provokes the question whether the work was therefore for God's eyes only?

Newell Post at foot of spiral staircase over the chancel arch

The Medieval Carvings of Halsall Church

A veiled woman

The medieval carvings of Halsall St Cuthberts have stood the ravages of time and weathering for well over 500 years. Some have disintegrated and others have lost fine detail. The sandstone, with which St Cuthbert's church is constructed, is not a particularly hard variety and so many of the carvings have done very well to survive acidic rain and the ever present south westerly winds blown in off the Irish sea and laden with sand and salt. The majority of the carvings adorn the chancel and among them are depictions of the seven deadly sins. It was believed in medieval times that all manner of demons and devils inhabited churches attempting to divert parishioners from pious ways. The carvings and gargoyles were created to frighten away these bad spirits. Another theory holds that the bad spirits were unable to enter inside a hallowed place and so masons depicted them sat on the outside leering down at church goers.

While some of Halsall's carvings are vile creatures, there are also sanguine heads of a knight, a fiddler, a greenman (an ancient pagan fertility symbol) and a bearded man. There is also a woman with flowing hair and a woman in a veil which is a wimple. It is possible to assume that these carvings may indeed be of locals who the master mason thought to include. Perhaps he was showing off his skill at capturing the features of a local character. Halsall's most distinctive carving is one of a man praying in a boat. There were two of these on opposite pinnacles of the eastern wall. One is ravaged beyond recognition the other has been restored in 1985 and is therefore a modern rendition of an ancient theme. The boat is representative of the church and the man represents the people. This is an image which was quite powerful and topical for the people of Halsall at this time, because Halsall was closer to the sea and its spire would have been a distinctive landmark for boats coming onto the shore or sailing up the Mersey.

There are no carvings on the nave the body section of the church. There are two possible reasons for this; one is that the nave belonged to the people and was somewhat a community hall so secular in comparison with the chancel, which was divine. The second reason is that there may have been plans to make the nave as ornate as the chancel but because it was completed after the black death of 1349 many of the skilled craftsmen were dead and others were scarce to tackle intricate work.

There are some carvings on the buttresses of the bell tower and also high up on the tower itself aligned with the four points of the compass. There is an angel to the north, a winged bull to the west a lion to the south and an eagle to the east. Inside the church there are many fine carvings in masonry and wood.

Whispering gargoyles

The Halsall Brass

The renovated brass

Halsall Church is the proud owner of an ancient brass dedicated to Henry Halsall and his wife Ann in 1589. The brass is listed in the definitive list of monumental brasses in the British Isles 1926. Dave Sephton (Churchwarden) was alerted to this by the Monumental Brass Society and a site meeting took place in October 2010. The brass is very intricate with lovely detail and comprises a crest in four quarters containing detail of dragon heads and a griffin sergeant sable. It also includes a six line foot inscription in English which is significant as most inscriptions were in Latin.

The outcome of the meeting and inspection was that the brass is being damaged by acids leeching in from the ancient stonework. It was necessary that the brass should be professionally restored. A specification was prepared to present to the Parochial Church

Council to agree that the brass, which was poorly mounted should be refurbished and remounted on a cedar board by rivets, giving more protection against theft and deterioration. Martin Sutchfield, consultant and expert on medieval brass, directed operations and our brass went to William Lack the foremost restorer of monumental brass in England for the work to be done. This work could only be done first by obtaining the permission from the diocese by securing a faculty and Eddie Carr, secretary of the PCC completed the necessary documentation. With the help of Eddie Carr and Dave Sephton an application for grant was made by myself and we secured two grants to cover the full cost of the work.

The outcome was that the brass was returned beautifully restored and mounted on cedar wood. The ancient and holy Church of St Cuthbert Halsall now has a valuable medieval monument displayed to best effect in the chancel. This will be secure and last for many more centuries.

The Carpenter's Grave

In the summer of 2011 a young university student Danielle Soper from York archaeological department, came to visit our church to study the chantry chapels for her dissertation on chantries in the North West of England. I pointed out some of the rare and wonderful features of our 700 year old medieval church, which was extremely interesting to Danielle. Outside in the churchyard I brought to Danielle's attention two slabs with etched crosses and she duly photographed them. I suggested they may have been altar stones.

Early in 2012 on a second visit, Danielle reported that the two stones were not altar stones.   Her tutor Dr Alexandra McLain, an expert in medieval gravestones, identified one stone as of 14th century origin, a straight armed cross with clustered foliate terminals. The cross is a stepped cross on three steps often called a Latin cross or Golgotha. The steps represent Calvary and the three steps to the cross, faith, hope and love. The work of Taylor and Radcliffe 1897 suggested that this stone was taken out of the chancel and was the tomb stone of Sir Francis Anderton. Francis Anderton was a Jacobite rebel who was imprisoned for two years and lived his days out at Lydiate Hall. He died in 1762 and was buried in Halsall Church. With the title 'Sir' we might have expected a tomb inscribed with the gentleman's name and details of his birth and death. However, Sir Francis Anderton was a Catholic and recognition on a grave in this way was forbidden. Moreover he had become impoverished due to recusant fines for being a Roman Catholic. It is plausible to believe his family did not have the means for a more elaborate stone. Halsall was now an Anglican church. My suggestion is that this carved 14th century stone was used to make the grave of Sir Francis anonymous and being very definitely a Catholic stone, would have fitted the purpose for an eminent personage such as Sir Francis.

Even more curiously, another stone 'in situ' next to the chancel was identified by Dr Mc Lain as of 15th century origin and contains a Calvary cross with cusping on the terminals of the cross arms. It also contains a carpenter's set square in L shape and a tri square. It was often usual to mark a tradesman's grave with the instruments of his profession. There are no words on the slab, but we must remember that back in the 15th century few people could read. The symbols of the tools of his trade were sufficient to mark his resting place. The situation of the grave, right next to the altar on the outside of the chancel suggests two things: first that the person was not noble or rich enough to be included inside the church, ie not a person of the gentry; secondly his role was important enough, however, to give him an elaborate gravestone and a prime position as a member of the laity as close to the chancel and altar as possible. He may well have been a local man. While the master mason would have had control over architectural design he was generally nomadic and would travel after finishing a job whereas a skilled carpenter could always find work locally. The master mason depended on his master carpenter to design and construct the frames around which the masons cut the stones to construct the arches which support the church and give it such depth and beauty. The master carpenter would also have created the framing for the four beautiful windows in the Chancel.

If this is so, the master carpenter may well have been a local man and the gravestone has remained undisturbed for several hundred years. The man may well have been a victim of the Black Death of 1349 and recognised for his valuable contribution to the edifice, by being laid to rest alongside the church he loved and on which he so painstakingly worked, close to the chancel which was his masterpiece.

The Carpenter's grave

The Glover Monument George Bullock 1810

The Reverend Glover Moore was the son of Nicholas Moore of Barton. He was born in 1736 and went to Oxford in 1856. He married a daughter of the celebrated Liverpool surgeon Thomas Antrobus and became curate of St Nicholas parish church of Liverpool. In 1778 he became Rector of Halsall and remained so until his death in 1809. After his death, his family had Glover Moore interred in the Chancel of the church and they commissioned a monument by the famous sculptor George Bullock. The monument is sculpted out of marble and it hangs on the north wall of the chancel. George Bullock was one of the most versatile and interesting artists of his day. He came to Liverpool in 1801 and in that year he exhibited 6 busts at the Royal Academy. His studio in Liverpool displayed all manner of furniture, lamps, mosaics and monuments in marble, bronze and stone. The monument which hangs in the chancel at St Cuthbert's is one of only five remaining monuments made by George Bullock. It is signed by him on the white marble oval. The beautiful green marble back slab is Mona Marble from Anglesey. Bullock raised his profile by establishing the Liverpool Academy. He died in 1818 at the young age of 35 and a portrait of him hangs in the Walker Art Gallery.

Howard Davies, an expert in sculpture of this period, visited our church in September 2011 to photograph and provide information on our monuments. We have 4 monuments 3 of which are clearly signed and dedicated to former Rectors. There is the Monument sculpted by Longfield and dedicated to Nathaniel Brownwell rector between the years 1684-1719. Another monument by Spence is dedicated to Richard Loxham rector 1916-1843 it is large and depicts grief in the form of a despairing woman. Daniel Sephton of Manchester created the monument to Anna Bold, daughter of the Lancashire MP Peter Bold; he was an eminent sculptor and artist he died 11 Feb 1759.

Halsall Churchwardens

Halsall church has a fairly accurate record of rectors dating back to the first millennium. It does not have a full record however of the churchwardens. They change far more frequently than the incumbent and many are lost in history,whilst others have some memorial set in stone or carving or maybe as a pen and ink reference.

The office of Churchwarden dates from the 13th Century and is a prestigious and time honoured role, within a parish, dating back to early medieval times. Their role has changed throughout history with increasing and decreasing responsibilities. Wardens have through the centuries cared for the church building, cared for the incumbents (Rectors, priests and curates) facilitated the services and provided a supportive role to the parishioners in changing times and religions.

The office of Churchwarden was not restricted to the wealthy classes. It was a sought after position and wardens generally served for a maximum of three years. A turnover of good men was essential and in a small village it required a head of household who was literate or at least numerate. They had to be able to compile lists and in the pre reformation times these lists included 'Peters pence' which was an ecclesiastical tax payable by every household of a farthing for the poor and a halfpenny for better off tenants. This was paid yearly at the annual visitation and passed on to Rome and the Pope.

Communal life in the parish made heavy demands on the villagers. They were not expected to be indifferent to the church or village customs. The church and priest were cared for by the parishioners and in turn the church cared for the souls of generations during their life and afterwards. The Churchwardens played their part by relieving the Incumbent of temporal concerns such as the fabric and maintenance of the church building. Wardens are the chief liaison between the Rector and the parish, they are responsible jointly with the Incumbent, for the care of all property of the Parish including the rectory and grounds ensuring that all property is kept in good repair and insured.

Wardens ensure that all church property is properly registered in the Land Titles Office, and that the deeds are in the possession of the Registrar of the Diocese. They also have the duty to ensure that any specific requirements with respect to maintaining a church's historic designation are dealt with in a timely and appropriate manner. This is particularly relevant in a medieval church like St Cuthbert's.

Churchwardens are also responsible for carrying out (or at least organizing) an annual inspection of the church building. They hold a key to the church and are entitled to access at any time. The grounds of the church also come under the purview of the Churchwardens,

There are also responsibilities in connection with the Sunday services which involve the input of Churchwardens. They ensure that any visitors or newcomers are welcomed and assisted. In this modern day they are also primarily responsible for health and safety.

The Halsall parish registers list all the churchwardens from 1606-1754. In this list we have many local names, including John Plumb who founded a local charity still presented by Downholland parish council. John Harker, whose bridge crosses the canal in Plex lane and John Segar one of many Segars who were proud to be Churchwardens. They were responsible for building drainage ditches so that the moss could be farmed. Their proud claim is that they have provided Churchwardens for Halsall from 1675 to the mid 18th century. Other typical Halsall names are present Blundell, Fazakerley, Mawdesley, Kenyon, Rimmer, Barton and Sephton to name but a few.

Churchwardens have often left a memorial of their time in stone or brass. Thus high up on the North side of the nave is a tablet with the names John Segar and Henry Yate 1700. Henry Park and Sam Pye have a brass plate in the vestry dated 1739. The service of Henry Harker is recorded on an engraved plaque at the back of the church. John Rymer and Joseph Owen have their graves marked with their service in 1751 and E Threlfall and T Ashcroft were the wardens for Queen Victoria's diamond jubilee with a stone, commemorating this event next to the Lych gate, put there in 1897. The service of John Grimshaw and Jack Huyton is recorded in Canon Bullough's book 1984. High up on the tower facing south are the names of Richard Hesketh and Robert Maudesley Churchwardens 1695 chiseled in stone. Others have their graves inscribed with the duty that they performed.

There are many churchwardens whose contributions are not registered physically and who are contemporaries to the memory. It is perhaps beholding on us to honour these persons by collating a list as was done so diligently in the 17th and 18th centuries.

All churchwardens and curates between the dates 1620-1754 are recorded in the parish registers. Below are wardens known outside those dates usually because there is some written or physical evidence of their term of office. The source is indicated where known.

1541 Robert Shurlacurs, Robert Wirral, Rogerus Pie, Edmundus Barton, George Fairclough, William Balshaw,
(Diocesan registers Chester)
1760 Thomas Kenyon, Roger Barton (Bullough A guide to Halsall Church)
1762 John Whitehead, Thomas Blundell (details carved on tower)

1811   T Halsall, E Blundell
1863   John Heaton, Peter Ackers (from church rate book)
1897   E Threlfall, T.Ashcroft (stone alongside lych-gate)
1934   W Threlfall, Harry Sergeant (bell ringing boards in the belfry)
1935   Job Grimshaw, Harry Sergeant
1938   JRimmer, Harry Core
1940   J Rimmer, G Bond
1944   W Gradwell, H Core
1947   W Gradwell, J Sephton (on church weathercock)
1948   J Sephton, W Gradwell
1951   James Sephton, William Leadbetter
1961   Harold Grimshaw, Henry Sergeant
1984   John Grimshaw, Jack Huyton, (Bullough)
1996   Doug Bonner, Reg Harris
2003   Tom Welch, Ron Thompson
2009   Brian Heaton, David Sephton
2013   Malcolm Sergeant, Brian Heaton

The 1808 Plan of Church and Grounds

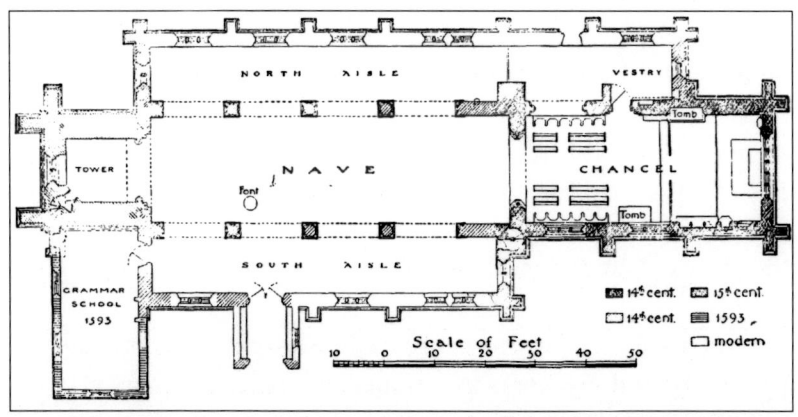

A church and grounds can alter dramatically over time and the church plan circa 1808 shows a much changed perspective to what we view today. The most striking feature of the plan of Halsall church and grounds circa 1808 is that it shows a much smaller church yard walled all around. The overall view of the church would have been to make it seem more on an incline and overall a more prominent landmark.

The plan is drawn to scale and shows several entrances, including one due east which might have served as an exit for coffins, which were stored in the hearse house at the extreme north east of the church. The hearse house has since been demolished. Another entrance opens south east onto Summerwood Lane and is the most elaborate of the entrances with high carved pillars. They appear, however, to be out of use because no path is evident to the church porch. The present day entrance is on a much shortened path as the boundary wall does not extend much beyond the grammar school and opens by a simple metal turnstile. It does not follow the course of the modern path, but instead veers further to the south. To the immediate right is a sundial, which is rectangular in base; this suggests it is the dial now positioned further east in the centre of the south facing churchyard. A small path leads from the porch entrance to the now bricked up doorway of the Grammar school, where the coat of arms of Edward Halsall is still visible but much eroded. It is probable that shortly before this plan was made the main road through to Scarisbrick was opened. Before this the church was passed by a road which went between the church and the post office along the depression now found next to the original wall in the enclosed church yard and crossed by two bridges.

The next interesting feature in the churchyard is the ancient baptismal font which is positioned next to the chancel. This has now been moved close to the church porch. The grave of Edward Segar of Barton is the only one shown with a metal railing surround. Local families all have their plots indicated; for example Blundell's ground, Hesketh's ground, Culshaw's ground etc. The land to the west of the church where now there is an extensive graveyard up to the main road was at that time empty, except for the grave of John Garner which lies in the south-west corner.

Many of the grave plots on the plan have since disappeared. There are very few graves today which are 17th century and hardly any from the 18th century. Many of the older stones were moved and some evidence can be found of these stones incorporated into paths. One such example is the stone which marks John Fazakerley's ground, this is now positioned outside the brick built out houses. The churchyard was extended to accommodate the growing population of the village in the 19th century and today the Victorian graves predominate. Several 18th century stones have been relocated, the most prominent being that of the rector Nathaniel Brownwell 1684-1719 who was buried in the chancel with his son. The stones for both were moved outside the church in 1873 when the floor was raised in the Chancel. They can now be found between the Grammar school and the Porch along with the memorial to Edward Segar curate who died in 1641. The stone of the Reverend John Stanley is situated between the buttresses at the North West corner of the church. He was rector 1750 and died in 1757

Another curious fact is the number of people buried inside the church. No doubt some pecking order prevailed so that a plot nearer the altar was the ultimate position. It was here that Nathaniel Brownwell and Nicholas Brownwell were laid before their stone was moved out of the chancel. We also have Henry Mordaunt, the rector from 1757 -1778 and Charles L Mordaunt the patron of Glover Moore the succeeding rector. Both are buried in the extreme corners of the chancel. The Victorian era heralded an expansion of the churchyard and today most of the older visible stones date from this period.

The Halsall Imp

The Halsall Imp

The Cathedrals of Chester and Lincoln both celebrate the medieval carving of an imp. Indeed, many medieval churches have grotesque carvings of gargoyles and hideous devils, but a solitary imp is very much rarer. These images are often positioned on the exterior buttresses or towers of the church and they represented the evil that lay outside the church forbidden to enter. They were a reminder to the faithful of the torments by demons that awaited any who fell out of favour with God.

Halsall church has many carvings in stone and wood. The images on the exterior of the 14th century building have taken a battering from the elements over the centuries and some are entirely defaced. However, Halsall too has an imp, a mischievous little creature with bony arms a small nose and a cheeky grin. He may have been a visual reminder to naughty medieval children that the devil takes many forms. His head and eyes have suffered from acid rain but you can still make out his bony arms and piggy nostrils.

The Halsall imp can be found on the south side of the church, the side on which the Sun shines and where the entrance porch is situated. He is at the altar end on the right arch of the large middle chancel window. He sits there, mocking passers-by and laughing at the Sun. He is in good company with other austere face carvings surrounding him. See if you can find him on your next visit to the church or set children the task of finding other strange carvings hidden in crevices on the church façade. Perhaps they could draw or photograph what they see before they are lost completely to erosion by the weather and pollution.

The Hangman

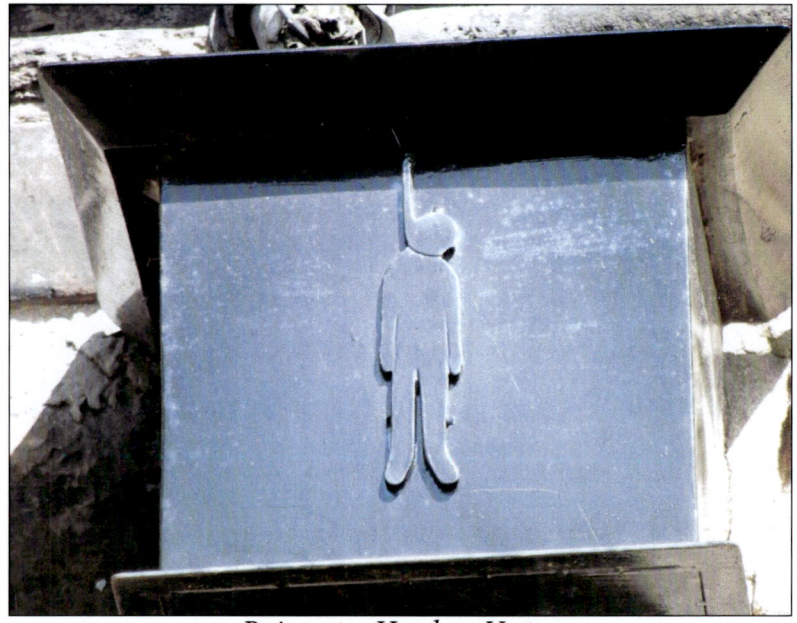

Rainwater Head on Vestry

Several parishioners have commented upon the effigy of a hanged criminal which adorns the new rainwater head on the vestry, replacing the previous item which was stolen for its metal content. Many have asked if it refers to local historical fact.

There never was in historical record a public hanging at Halsall. However vigilante groups did take it upon themselves to enact their own summary justice in times past. One such occasion occurred around the end of the 18th century. There was a girl in service at Halsall hall whose name is lost but whom we shall refer to as Catherine Gorsuch. She was a descendant of another Catherine Gorsuch who survived the Black Death four centuries earlier. Catherine lived in a cottage tied to Gorsuch farm and daily made her way to and from her home to work at Halsall Hall for Colonel Mordaunt. The woods which presently extend to the ruins of the ancient rectory behind the church extended much further along Gorsuch lane to Morris Lane and Catherine became wary that during her journey home she was being watched by a presence lurking in the woods. As darkness fell in the November of 1796 Catherine's journey, in fading light, became ever more anxious because she was convinced she was being stalked. She let her fears be known and village folk, alert to all the comings and goings in the village, let their suspicion fall on Hugh from Barton. Hugh wasn't the brightest of men he was a 'gibberer' who couldn't talk properly and he was simple minded. He got excitable around ladies and most warded him off with a severe word. He had a fancy for Catherine and often followed her around during church processions and at the annual fayre. Hugh was put under the supervision of the curate and made to tidy the churchyard for several nights. It was during one of these nights that Catherine Gorsuch was attacked and indecently assaulted. The offence took place near the old ancient vicarage and Hugh startled the attacker with a shout. Her attacker escaped up New Cut lane in the direction of the newly opened canal and there he was apprehended, boarding a narrow boat on route to Wigan. John Cheshyre was not from these parts but had been moored nearby for several weeks doing repair to canal banks and bridges. Locals hung him upside down by his ankles over the canal bridge near to the new public house called the Saracens Head before letting him fall head first into the soft mud and clay.

The present effigy of a hanged figure is the wishful thinking of one of the churchwardens who feels that this type of justice would be' right and fitting' for the thieves who have been stealing lead of the church roof and who stole the original rainwater head for its metal content.

It is interesting, that in this day and age people still find time to notice addition and alteration to church structure. The medieval gargoyles and other carvings were made to be noticed and to convey a message about demons and angels and about those who defend the church and those who are outside of the church.

Migrant workers on Halsall Farms

In the present day it is not uncommon to find many eastern European migrant workers helping out on the farms in and around Halsall and West Lancashire. Indeed, they are continuing a practice which was started by the Irish in the late 18th century when seasonal workers made the journey from the west of Ireland to these parts to supplement their meagre standard of living at home. Many came to dig the canals and railway cuttings as navvies and their efforts are commemorated with the statue on the canal by the Saracen's Head. Other Irish migrants fulfilled the role of farm labourers at a time when there was a hungry demand from growing populations in the industrial towns in Lancashire during the Industrial revolution.

Many of the seasonal Irish workers came back time and again to the same farms and became regular visitors. They worked and were fed and housed on the farms and their legacy is the 'paddy house' or 'shant'. This is a small outbuilding which acted as a dwelling and was sometimes purposely built. There are examples on many farms, for instance, Hesketh Farm on Station Road. The Irish workers frequented the local pubs at the weekend and attended the local church usually at 'Our Lady' in Lydiate because the majority were Catholic. They were often reticent to enter the pews which they thought were reserved for locals and stayed standing at the back during the services.

Patrick McGing is now 99 years of age and lives in Kinuary in County Mayo near Westport. In an interview for a local publication he recalls how he first came to England in 1932 and followed established connections, because his father Michael had already been over before him. He came to an estate farm at Barton house, where the work started in late spring, planting large areas of vegetables and then tending them before harvesting in September. They would also save hay during the summer months. Usually they worked in pairs and for 11 hours a day. He describes most of his employers as being very nice men; he worked for John Rimmer, Dick Cropper at Halsall Hall farm and Jack Harrison 'the goose king' at Mill House farm. He emphasised, "You had to pull your weight at Barton House or they would let you go". Whilst having a drink in the Scotch Piper one Saturday night, the parish priest sent a drink over to Patrick and said, "I worked with that man today and I did not know a man could work so hard." In the 1960's when he came over the work was less physical because of mechanization and the hours had been reduced also. The seasonal workers were careful with their money, knowing it was essential to enable their families to exist through the winter in Ireland, so they sent their wages home by registered post. Patrick continues, "I usually earned about 35 shillings a week (£1.75) plus board and lodgings". Sometimes a frequent visitor would be given a skilled job and the father of our own churchwarden Dave Sephton, working at White House farm employed an Irishman John McGing who became a trusted employee and family friend and stayed permanently on the farm. When he became ill through an accident he was afforded all the rights of sickness pay and holiday pay and had his own 'paddy house' at White house farm. Increased mechanization and Ireland's entry into the EU has meant very few Irish workers come over now and their place has been taken by migrant workers from Eastern Europe. However their contribution has been invaluable to the economic prosperity of this area.

(reference Killawalla Co Mayo: Home and Away 2010)

Music at Halsall Church through the ages

The present Halsall Church dates from 1310. The early structure has been added to and built on, not just for spoken office and prayer, but also for musical praise. In the 14th century the early building consisted of a nave and a much smaller chancel. At this time worship was a passive exercise and singing would be confined to the priest, who was required to sing the office. There would be no congregational participation. The plainsong and chant sung by trained choirs would more often be heard in the abbeys and monasteries such as that at Burscough.

Did the monks of Burscough ever visit and sing in Halsall? It is conjecture but after the ravages of the Black Death were over towards the end of the 14th century, Halsall entered a period of stability. The new chancel was constructed and was finished about 1400. It was one of the most beautiful chancels in England and we may imagine the monks of Burscough, curious to see its splendour, came to sing parts of the mass. There remains to this day a possible link between our beautiful medieval choir benches in the chancel and the closure of Burscough Abbey in 1543. It is thought that they were rescued from the plunder which followed the closing of the monasteries.

Under the Tudors, England enjoyed a golden age of music, composers such as Thomas Tallis William Byrd and John Shepard, created polyphonic masterpieces interweaving intricate sacred text into song. This music rivalled and ranked with the greatest music of Italy and Spain. Much of this music needed a trained choir and it is doubtful that Halsall would ever have experienced the magnificent opulence of this music. It would have been heard in the Cathedrals, however, and Halsall at this time was in the diocese of Lichfield which was 80 miles away..

With the coming of the Reformation, Martin Luther claimed that a hymn is praising God a thousand times more than the spoken prayer. He wanted music to be an active rather than a passive affair for the parishioners. The Reformation sought to take the mystery out of music and make it a form of worship with which the layperson could identify; it was also to be in English not Latin. Congregational chant claimed Luther was the gift of the Reformation to the lay parishioner, by allowing participation in the service by singing psalms and antiphons. He advised that the music should only allow one note to each word. This would simplify it and move away from grandiose motets such as 'Spem in Alium' by Thomas Tallis, which contains only 31 words yet took 14 minutes to completely sing.

We know that Halsall and the region of south west Lancashire clung fiercely onto the Catholic faith and change was often slow to implement Reformation principles. Few people could read text even in English and fewer could sing. If congregational chant were to happen it would have to be led by the minister singing one part and the parishioners repeating. One effect the Reformation did have was that elaborate Catholic polyphony was not lost but was performed in secret. It was not performed in chapels because they became illegal under Elizabeth I,instead the music went to the great houses like Rufford, Speke and Lydiate, where choirs would meet to perform and this became a means of keeping the mass alive in Lancashire.

While the Book of Common Prayer makes provision for sung service, the chance of any unaccompanied singing at Halsall before the Restoration of Charles II was unlikely. Puritans within the Cromwellian regime considered music in church to be the work of the devil and for the duration of the Commonwealth 1640-1666 music was banned. The Restoration allowed the Church of England to re establish and stabilize itself. It became receptive to Baroque influences of composers such as Mozart, Bach and Schubert and music took on a greater importance for Anglican church services. However this again was largely confined to Cathedrals. In the rural parish church in the 18th century music was often performed in a western gallery. Halsall may have had such a gallery, but there is no structural evidence of this. The gallery was where fiddles and reed pipes may have accompanied the singing of a small choir. The coming of the church organ meant the end for such western gallery choirs and this is depicted very descriptively in Thomas Hardy's novel 'Under the Greenwood Tree'. The novel starts on Christmas Eve as the choir get together to celebrate Christmas, against the backdrop of the imminent coming of an organ. This is perceived as a fatal blow to their choir. The music of a western gallery was of a more folky type and often considered not solemn enough for church service and one ponders the extent to which such a gallery would have been used at Halsall.

When 'Hymns Ancient and Modern' was published, it was adopted by high church Anglicans. The 19th century and the Victorian era in particular, was the heyday for Anglican church music. The participation of the congregation envisaged by Luther some 400 years earlier came to fruition. The music at Halsall was accompanied by an organ installed in 1873 in memory of Richard B H Benson Halsall, patron of Halsall. Originally this was hand blown but electrified later and was replaced with the present instrument in 1964. The 'English Hymnal' was published in 1906 for the Church of England under the editorship of Percy Dearmer and Ralph Vaughan Williams. Arrangement of hymns by such esteemed composers facilitated the singing of hymns in church to become the popular form of worship it is today.

Choir practice on a moon lit night

A Halsall Ghost Story

It was a sombre day, twenty four days after the winter solstice and one of those January days when it never becomes properly light. The threatened forecast of rain all day had not disappointed the ducks. The cloud layer stayed low and threatening and the wind swirled the leaves around the churchyard and on to the paths.

It is always autumn in the Halsall churchyard. The evergreens shed copious amounts of leaves all year round and they lay side by side with the dead. Today, they stuck to the damp paths as the street lights lit up early and the light faded on the moss. In the north part of the churchyard it is even darker and no one was about. The descending gloom hovered over the tombstones and I contemplated whether this was the perfect moment for the dead to make contact with the living, and why not here in a medieval churchyard? I wait and watch but even the wildlife stays mute and hidden. Nothing is evident, even less a phantom moving through the trees.

A few years back a dog walker claimed to have seen a spirit shape moving in the woods near the old rectory. I walk through the churchyard scarcely able now to read the inscriptions on the stones. The wind roars through the tops of the pines and the bell tolled the parting knell with a discordant note due to one bell cord being frayed. Eventually I take rest on a seat in the garden. It is slightly damp and a shiver courses the length of my tired body. In his book 'These charming acres' Peter Nodin alludes to a grey lady whose tomb rests in the north wall of the chancel for she wanted to be buried neither inside nor outside the church. Her ghostly face is reported to have been seen high up on the south chancel wall. Perhaps the dog walker had caught sight of this restless apparition? However there is no trace of this noble lady on this winter eve. The conditions seem perfectly conducive but the curtain between this world and the next is firmly closed. I leave the churchyard when only a glimmer of the fading day remains. The damp has sent a chill to reach my bones and my steps are weary.

In the night as I sleep a long, long disturbed sleep my dreams are dominated by thoughts of this division between life and death. The night is endless and as it continues on the more desperate I am to penetrate this curtain and find a way through. A panic sets in but my heart is not racing. When will the darkness end? My arm eventually forces through in desperation and grasps to hold something, anything and I feel a fist full of leaves as my hand pushes through the green grass.

*A shadow falls over the tomb of
Richard Halsall. Might this be the Grey Lady?*

The Chorister

(A tribute to an Anglican lady)

The hymn books are open; the bell peals are still
The choir processes the chancel to fill
And you're there in amongst them with countenance rare
Voice of an angel and sun on your hair
The assembly is still now in medieval pew
And I am strategically placed to see you
To hear your melissima antiphon chant
Magnificat te deum requiescant
 The reredos is shining each crocketed spire
In decorated formation is there to admire
The bells in your votives, the chimes in your octaves
At the head of the choir

It's matins in February
Sunbeams slanting in
Through perpendicular stained glass
Of etched seraphim
The sedilla are full now the nave is sold out
To yesteryears ancestors dying to shout
Their applause to the rooftops for the hymns they have heard
Motets and acapella of Tallis and Byrd

Finials and pinnacles ascend to their Lord
As your voice like the lark is sent heavenward
And tingles the stars and the spines of the blessed
While the hour is struck by the clock in the west

Your tone is illuminate
Like manuscript capitals
Your psalms iridescent and sound like sung gospels
You should see her, the chorister
A sight to behold
You must see her resplendent in purple enrobed
And as you retire in recessional refrain
The angels audit every echo and strain
And your flowers are smiling and the stones hold acclaim
And your voice ever lingers and will always remain.

Stephen Henders

Halsall Church Timeline

1320	Norman wooden church demolished work begins on stone church.
1340	Nave built
1350	Chancel completed rebuilding starts on Nave
1360	Old Rectory built
1420	Nave completed with north and south aisles.
1520	Clerestory window installed.
1539-49	Rood screen dismantled.
1559	Chantry chapels suppressed
1589	Halsall brass made
1593	Grammar school added (Now choir vestry)
1606	Parish registers begun (incomplete)
1662	Compulsory parish register starts
1692	Draining of Martin Mere begins
1717	New rectory built to the west of the church
1725	Sundial placed in churchyard
1751	North and south aisles rebuilt
1780	Bells recast
1790	Road opened in front of the church,
1808?	Church plan of burials inside and outside church.
1811	Bells inscribed
1827	Clock installed
1841	St Thomas's built
1847	Old rectory pulled down
1850	Ground plan of Halsall Church.
1852	Spire rebuilt
1861	School transferred from vestry to Halsall Hall.
1871	St Thomas' a parish in own right.
1873	Organ installed and Chancel floor lowered.
1886	Large scale renovation and Nave roof timbers replaced.

1895	Mission at Barton (St Oswald erected)
1906	New rectory built by Canon Blundell
1931	Bells recast
1948	Bishop of Warrington orders removal of Col Blundell's sword from south aisle wall.
1951	Lych gate constructed.
1965	New organ installed.
1985	Biblical inscription below clerestory window restored.
2006	Clock refurbished and reinstated
1/11/2008	Church becomes part of United Benefice with St Thomas's Lydiate and Downholland.
2013	Church closed temporarily in December because of unsafe spire.

England's Timeline

1307	Edward the Confessor dies.
1349	Black Death his North West England May-June
1349	
1381	The Peasant's Revolt
1415	Agincourt
1455-1485	War of the Roses
1483	Battle of Bosworth
1509	Henry VIII crowned
1529	Henry severs links with Rome and becomes Head of the church in England.
1534	Act of Supremacy.
1536	Dissolution of the monasteries.
1536	Pilgrimage of grace (Northern Rebellion)
1549	First Prayer Book
1559	Act of Uniformity
1560	Suppression of mystery plays.
1553	Mary I restores Catholicism.
1558	Elizabeth I restores Protestantism.
1581	Treason to convert to Catholicism
1587	Execution of Mary Queen of Scots
1588	Spanish Armada.
1605	Gunpowder Plot.
1642	English Civil War.
1649	Execution of Charles I
1649-1660	Commonwealth and Protectorate under Cromwell
1660	Charles II restored as Monarch.
1662	Act of Uniformity.
1688	Glorious Revolution.
1701	Act of Settlement.
1707	Act of Union

1815	Napoleonic Wars.
1829	Catholic Relief Act
1834	New Poor Law
1846	Corn Laws Repealed
1846	Great Hunger in Ireland
1870	Education Act
1914-18	First World War
1939-45	Second World War

Resources

Bullough H (1985)   A guide to Halsall and its Church.

Budden C W (1929)   Ancient Churches of the Liverpool
                        Diocese, Liverpool Diocesan

Cox E W (1896)   Notes on Halsall Church   Historic
                        Society of Lancashire and Cheshire

Duffy E   (1992)   The Stripping of the Altars Yale Univ
                        Press

Gibson T E (1876)   Lydiate Hall and its Associations
                        Ballantyne Hanson & Co

Hatcher J (2008)   The Black Death Phoenix

Hilton J A (1994)   Catholic History of Lancashire,
                        Phillimore

Nodin P (1936)   These Charming Acres

Pearce J P (1931)   Romantic Tales of Old Lancashire,
                        Ormskirk Advertiser

Strong R   (2008)   A little History of the English Country
                        Church, Vintage

Taylor H & Radcliffe   Notes on Halsall Church, Historic Soc
R   D   (1896)   of Lancs, Cheshire

                        The Victoria History of the County
                        of Lancashire (1906)   Archibald
                        Constable & Co